T0349264

SECONDARY WORLDS

AARON GEDALIAH

PREFACE

In 1967, W.H. Auden gave a series of lectures in honor of T.S. Eliot in which he described works of art as "secondary worlds". For him, humans have two fundamental desires. The desire to know the truth of the given or "primary world" that lies outside ourselves. Just as important is our desire to create worlds of our own. Ones of inherent value that entice our imagination. A world both enchanted and sacred.

The idea of secondary worlds has been with me many years. Shortly after writing "The False God's Lullaby", I decided to focus on secondary worlds as a topic for many of the poems in this collection. In addition to these themes, I've continued to write about "the human condition" with candor, and perhaps more than a little artistic license. I've done so to convey experiences I think many of us have, but only reluctantly do we share them in moments of vulnerability.

My desire to pursue this has many fathers. Among them are Franz Kafka's experiences with despair "noting down what we see among the ruins", Rainer Maria Rilke's confession that "we are most ignorant about what is most our own" and James Baldwin's stark honesty that "we are afraid to reveal ourselves because we trust ourselves so little."

But we are most afraid of what paleontologist Loren Eisley called the "dark murmur that arises from the abyss beneath us." What Sigmund Freud called Id ("The It") and Jacques Lacan called "the strange". D.H. Lawrence experienced it as "strange gods who come forth from the dark forest." But despite our turmoil, the chaos and futility we experience, the philosopher Will Durant spoke of something indispensable within us, if we could "but decipher our own souls". That life's mission is to "transform into light and flame all that we are or meet with." Much of what follows is written in that spirit.

Aaron Gedaliah

San Francisco, California

June 15th 2024

Table of Contents

REFLECTIONS, MOODS (PART 1)

WHO AM I?

(1)

I am not my thoughts,
but only the source
from where they move
through me.
Moment to moment,
ebb and flow,
random chatter among
my many selves,
clamoring for their say.
But only *the guided voice*
can silence them
(for a time),
when I strive to create
the indivisible one.
The illusion I aspire
for the world to see.

(2)

I am not my feelings.
I do not generate them
nor set their cadence,
nor direct their motion.
I only float among them.
Surrendering to their color,
when they come to rest
in lolling waves.
Whether they linger
or swiftly pass by,
is beyond my control.

Turbulences are never
far away,
rumbling
their discontent
before they rage.
I can do no more
than ride the storms,
deflect their fury
for a moment, as
I become the parent
within my mind,
soothing the frightened
child lost,
within my night.

I tell no one of my weakness.
The dark spells
that strangle me,
when I keep myself
from myself,
in moments of surging joy.
Listening to the voice that says:
Happiness in not yours to hold!

(3)

I'm not my behavior,
although others say it's so.
I'm its master and director,
and truth be told, that's
merely vain conceit.

There are others within me
stronger than my thoughts.
Hijackers who degrade
the cultivated one,
The one I wish to portray.
They resurrect the
rebellious child I'd hoped
to leave behind.

The unavoidable truth
is the animal in whom
I reside.

We're all frustrated creatures,
our hearts
will not concede.
Decorum
is simply the way
we get along in
the world outside.

(4)

There lies within me
someone underneath,
who slowly grew
over the years.

Watching
Noticing
Digesting
all experiences
I've forgotten, and
seem no longer
mine.

Among unseen remembrances
stirring beneath the surface,
are the undertow of
secrets about a secret.
Elusive things
refusing
to be buried.
An evasiveness
beyond my grasp.
It's silence guides me
whenever
I'm not looking.

(5)

I've come to know adulthood
as a fanciful lie, suppressing
my unhappy past.
Disfigured memories rise
like fairytale creatures.
Stirrings and callings from
a dark forest.

Past is never past.
The frictions of the world
summons the demons
I carry with me.
Uncertainty, anger, shame
rise and dictate
the course of my day.

In the worst of storms
I hide in sanctuary,
where no-one can see.
The diatribes I hide inside.
Ugly maelstroms of the past
rising in my throat,
until I vomit out myself
in rage against
what never changes.
Nor can I close the door
to its fury.

Yet all storms recede,
having had their say
(for a while).
So I again reweave
my *Self* into who
I've longed to be.

(6)

It's puzzling I can't experience
The I experiencing *me!*
My unity emits no sensation.
Just a vapor meandering
in and out
of awareness.

Thinking is just a
muffled humming inside
my head.

The *I* observes my many selves
as subject.
Listening as a neighbor would,
to a quarreling family
through thin walls.

I is a *meta-identity,*
looming above
the shapeshifters
I send into the world:
musician and poet
son and sibling
lover and friend
madcap and mensch.

(7)

Words murder what they name.
Me
I
Self
Identity.
Which of them describe
the elusive one?
The One
I perceive as simply
Being.
My words confuse as often
as they illuminate.
Ping-off one another
as often as letting me
peer within.

And yet without *you!*
Without other's ideas and
all the images and commotions
of the outside world,
who would give me form?
I'd merely be a voiceless
It — a being without
meaning or purpose.

And so I cannot be without
so many lures and confusions.
Sewn from strands of others
whom I've invited in
to play.
The mirrors and icons
that became the
ever-changing Pantheon
of my Identity.

(8)

The client sits across
from the therapist,
who must parry and thrust
against the obstinate *Me* —
the tedious and evasive one.
Hinting but never quite saying.

She, the patient one,
an unchanging presence
of calm and sanctuary.
Always seeking to understand
the disunion and dynamics,
of my many beings.
The ones who often lie,
and lie beneath my
poses and moods.
My blind motives and
cryptic utterances.

Until the *I* that *I am*
can trust *her,*
and begin to step
tenuously,
out into the open.

And like a magician
(who I am not),
She sees more clearly
who *I am.*
But just the same,
the essence of
        I
remains unseen.

ALURE OF A WOMAN

(1)

A woman's true beauty evades the
irrepressible momentum of youth.
Strutting plumages hailing
their glorious arrival.
Her beauty is revealed
in stillness when she closes
herself to the world outside,
and her soul travels
elsewhere.
A sereness found
in chance encounters.

Riding the subway during
a cold evening's commute.
She sits quietly across the aisle,
exuding something faraway.
Bundled in a Kelly-green coat,
lush chestnut hair flowing
down her shoulders.
Lost in a book.
Lost in herself.

Another young woman
happily absorbed in writing.
Her face hidden beneath
raven curls.
Beneath the desk
her legs sway gently
back and forth,
reliving a child's
rapturous moments merged,
with the pendulous cadence
of a high-arching swing.

More poignant than all
is a mature woman's beauty,
found in subtle longing
within her eyes.

She slowly strolls
through museum galleries,
and pauses for a time.
Suspended in the mirror
of another's beauty,
who knowingly
gazes back.

(2)

For an undistracted man
looking intently upon
her quiet beauty,
she becomes for him
a mistaken evocation
of a wordless promise
never made.

Something ancient beyond
his grasp.
A desire to find once more
a completeness
no woman has promised,
and none
can nourish.

The long-sought embrace
he imagines will raise him
into timeless rapture.

Condemned to live among
lures arising everywhere.
He wanders a vast field
of wildflowers,
perishing
in early bloom.

LULLABY

My first apartment was
near a Eucalyptus forest.
On summer nights
I slept with open windows,
so the breeze would bring
me the scented fog's release
into the down-world
of dreams.
Lulled by the distant
foghorn that guards
the Golden Gate.

In mornings I'd awaken
to its lonely *OM*
that watched over
my dreams.

Reassuring like a mother
who'd stayed through
the night,
softly cooing
to keep her child in
the realm of sleep.

THE STARDUST RAIN OF BLUES

Blue jazz fills my grey mind
on a rainy day,
when a cold front moves onshore
and rain drums down
on the window pane.

The restless dog of my mind
hounds for a walk in the park.
Hoping to wash away
Edward Hopper's image
of a man sitting alone,
in a Greenwich Village
Nighthawk café.

Stardust.
Kind of Blue.
Afro Blue Impressions.

Coltrane and Davis keen the
deadness of a tedious afternoon.
A muted trumpet's high pain.
The plaintive response of a tenor sax.
Soft, tentative phrases from
a lonely piano.
And the slow pulse of a string bass,
reminding my heart not
to slip away.

And so I soothe my angst
in the cool slow drips
of fading rain.
As cars hiss by melding
with the music of
Stardust.
Kind of Blue.
Afro Blue Impressions!

ANGEL OF LA RAMBLA

(for Karen Valderrama)

In a dark corner of La Rambla,
a lithe woman transforms herself
into an angel.
Cast in wings and robes
of black and silver,
she slowly mounts her throne.

Majestic and motionless,
eyes closed to the
clamorous flutter of
a crowded evening,
a serenity of stillness.
A tourist ambling by
stops to gaze at her.
She stirs within him
an urge to make
an offering.

Awakened
she looks down in silence
and sees emptiness.
Her finger runs across
his brow as she guides
his hand to her lips, and
bestows her blessing.

A regal smile breaks upon
her face,
as she gently
releases him.
Her head and hand
slowly raised to
the night sky,
she sends a blessing
to the heavens.

As she recedes into stillness
her eyes closing down,
In her presence he becomes
less empty.
And in those moments
that turn into days,
he feels her lingering
grace.

MAD STREET POETS OF HAIGHT-ASHBURY

The mad are
an illusory opera
of their own despair,
and each tortured soul
sings from the abyss
they carry with them.

I cross the street
to avoid their rants
to the wind and leaves,
and the traffic moving
swiftly by them.

I sometimes listen closely
to what they say.
Their raving madness is
a voice less stale,
less alienated
from themselves.
A poignancy surpassing
the truth of what
opaque poetry
often brings.

Curses and confusions,
laments and howling
at others not there,
who long ago sunk
a dagger
in their soul,
and still
twist the blade.

The rawness of
failed lives whose
unreality more real
than we could bare.
So we push them out
of our minds
and walk away,
as we would
the tormented
crying-out of
a wounded animal.

Because they scream
secrets for all to hear.
A madness touching
something
we cannot say.

Their yowling warns
us go no further
inside ourselves.

Do not go within the
most ancient of
dark feelings,
that approach you on
your loneliest night.

Because imagination
disguised as memories,
may push you down
into a blackness,
so far from the surface
you may never find
your way back.

WHEN ALANIS MORISETTE BECAME GOD

When Alanis Morrisette became God,
homesick Bartleby wept
in hopelessness and defeat.
And for a moment, I too felt
like a lost child sobbing,
before the power of
overwhelming goodness,
longing to be in its embrace.
Finding a sense of absolution,
though I've never done
egregious wrong.

When Alanis Morrisette became God,
I was as I am, a quiet atheist
comfortable with my biodegradable soul.
Just trying to follow a righteous path
(as best I could).

When Alanis Morrisette became God,
it was her smile and compassion that touched me.
And as I held-back surprised tears,
I remembered what a wise man
taught me.
Religion is from the Latin
Religare: to reconnect.

Religare holds the secret
when once we dwelled
in union, with a *Being*
we lost long ago.

And so our *orphaned souls*
wander endlessly
trying to fuse with our
primal myth.

For believers and non-believers,
to *re-connect* echoes
an ancient desire,
to feel once more,
More Than!
The splendor within
and beyond ourselves.

So even I,
a non-believer,
yearn for the arms of
Alanis Morrisette —
when she became God.

TIME PASSES
THROUGH US

SIGHTED BLINDNESS

So much of life hastily passes by.
Low winter light in the park
illuminates the sated grass.
Twirling yellow leaves falling,
as a young dog runs
to retrieve her ball.
Simple, unbounded joy!

Her owner heaves the ball,
never looking up from
his 3-by-6 wasteland.

A mother in a digital trance
sits on a park bench,
as her child runs
pure circles
of exuberance.

So many moments lost in
the deadness of
a contrived world.
Oblivious to what is real.

A guitarist plays an impassioned
serenade for
no one in particular.
Flowing grace of dancers rehearsing.
An elderly man smiling upon
the simplicity of his
precious days.
Life passes through us quietly,
always taking away
what's never noticed,
leaving what's spent behind.

And in the low of winter,
yellowed leaves scatter
in the fading light.

STANDING STILL

This life that passes by
once had meaning and purpose.
Faith in contentment found
at journey's end.

But as time fades
a moment arrives,
when the familiar withers
and the known life
is stunned,
by the indifference
of all that's new,
hell-bent
on leaving me
behind.

A gust and a blur.
The coldness of
inconsolable autumn.
Fallen leaves move towards
me in a flurry,
murmuring something
profound.

But I refuse to understand.

AN OLD ROAD

A long journey's weathered road
has faded memory.
Perhaps some are only
Things that I've
imagined.

Faintest among them
was riding up to camp
on a slender road,
wending through the forest.

Now I drive the wider highway.
I can still see remnants
of my past.
Knowing it wasn't a dream.
But sadly,
still devoured by
Nature's indifference.

Asphalt crumbling between
the trees and tall grasses.
Traces of the old passage
disappear
into the distance.
For which there is no destination,
and no return.

SKETCH OF MY FATHER

Across the boat house windows
my father has strung a cord.
So I cannot open the sweltered
room to the night's breeze.

The open camp's stone fireplace
is now blocked off.
So I cannot journey back to
those magical summer nights
when snarling flames popped
and a plume of sparks rose
into the deep blue of night.

My father has locked every door
that was opened to my youth.
My boyish anger seeps away
(having no container), only
a pang of softness remains
for his quiet torment.

Harsh eyes that once met mine
with such disapproval,
now colored only with sadness.

So many unwanted things
a father gives his son.
Boxes of enigmas a boy
cannot open.
So he entombs them
in a dark cellar.

Slowly disinterred with
the passing years,
I've conceded my scars
and counted the cost.
Those judgements cast
by a harrowed god
who once loomed over me.

My father now walks with a limp.
His dominant presence withered
by unforgiving years.

After dinner he sits outside
in the dark.
Away from the family bustle.
Huddled over his dessert,
he eats alone
in silence.

THE MEMORY WARD

I and my inmates are the ghostly
ones left behind.
Our beloved abandoned us,
leaving only their shells to waste away.
They were the bark of
mortal trees who died
much faster than we.

My beloved was a difficult partner.
Lost in fathoming existence:
the *what, why and where*
should we be going?
I was the clarity of feeling.
Lacking words to comfort him,
in his moments of despair.

I was root, trunk, and branch
to his chattering leaves.
A presence whose language
was sensations.

Now I am alone among
the other empty beings.
We haunt the day rooms,
and wander the halls with
only one feeling that remains.
This is not my home!

And so I patiently wait
for what my departed
always feared.
But each slow day
of dying
I plead to him.
Come back for me!

Like other roamers of the void,
who've escaped into the night.
My beloved returned to me
in a moment of clarity.

It wasn't always like this!
Once we vibrated with life in
a time and place so long ago.
We need to find our way
back home!

Sneak out of here if you can,
when no one else will see,
and I'll tell you how
to find your way.

Wander out in any direction
It does not matter where.
And do not fear the cold
who is your friend.
The full moon will be there
to guide you back in time.

I'll meet you once again
when you've arrived,
where all that was familiar,
the love that was,
the shelter of our
childhood home
will greet us.

And when you cross
the threshold,
I'll take your hand once more.
With our last step and breath
together,
we'll merge with the night
and enter
our final rest.

THE LONG NIGHT

Sheppard me across the long night,
for it's good not to be alone
in this waiting room.

Say my final goodbye to
memory's spindled tree, and
all the days I let slip by
through careless fingers.

Ferry me across these last hours
cradled in your embrace.
Just once more let me relive
the lightness of lost moments.
And let one bloom be
the final image I ever see.

Bring me back to the gentleness
of that April morning.
To hear once more
the slow moaning branch
above the child's swing.

A little boy in egg shell blue
lost in his blissful rhythmic sway.
Breathing in the sweetness of
earth and grass rising
in the morning's dew.

Hold me tight these last moments,
the passage scares me so.
I fear the silence beyond breathing.
The cold shudder of its embrace.

So let my final image be the sweetness
of that April morning and
know them all
no more.

WHISPERS

A child's mind naturally hears
the hidden within,
and bathes in its delights.
So begins our second birth,
destined to perish too soon.

As years pass by we are fated
to move beyond
our many sorrows.
But never freed from
the grasp of disenchantment.

Fantasies nourished us
when life was simple and
filled with possibility.
But as we journey further,
the chill of time
loosens fantasy,
and slowly it fades away.

And in those arid moments
wandering among shards
of our past,
we try piecing together
the mosaic of our dreams.

Fantasy was a whisper of
what could never be,
and yet we held to
the sweetness of its purity.
The echoes from a distant life,
are now the solace for
our diminished days.

AN UNEXPECTED DREAM

The sweetness of a dream
I dreamed of you last night.
Despite all the time that's lost,
the quiet who remains unseen
has held you close.

Remembrances of our
tentative dance.
The gambits we played when
no one else was looking.
Breaking smiles
and brightened eyes,
every time we passed
each other by.
Our idle chatter laced with
come-hither hints, leading
to the anxious night we met
in a quiet bar.

Words suddenly vanished
in beaming eyes.
Impatient to feel the flow
of sensations spiraling up
into our animal voices.

This morning I awake and go
about gray habits.
Yet I'm followed by a softness,
that feels like your breath
upon my neck.
Recalling moments of
aliveness felt long ago,
when your passion turned
to me.

IN THE SHADOW
OF EVIL

THE MARK OF CAIN

We who rise above all others,
long in memory,
deep in thought and reason,
apprehend
the *heart of darkness*
that is our creaturely past.

When undistracted we feel,
the relentless current dragging
us down to the cataract
of our demise.

In the cradle of primal memory
are frenzied-legacies of
a distant past.
Even chimpanzees roam
the borders of their domain
hunting and murdering
neighboring clans.

The *Mark of Cain* runs deep.

Before stepping into the East River
to drown his despair,
Spaulding Grey spoke of
blood-lust legacies
we've unleashed.
Germany, Russia, Cambodia.
To which there are
so many more.
A list too long for
any poem to bear.

Evil spews into the world.
He called it a menacing
cloud of insanity searching
for a place to descend.
Now has come our time
(once more)!
An estranged culture
drowning
in despondency.
A hopelessness stoked
by fear and hate.
We suffer our distractions
and refuse to see what
comes at us.

SERMON FOR AN IMPROBABLE CREATURE

(1)

We are all descendants of
a cursed race.
An improbable creature.
A rare mutation created
a chimpanzee-variant,
who arose
millions of years ago.
Fated to someday
takes its place
above the constraints
of the Natural Order.

Symbolic and loving.
Magical and spiritual.
Fearful and wrathful.
A calculating creature
blessed and cursed,
cleaved into
mind and instinct.

Its goodness weak and
easily betrayed.
That which isn't,
darkened by distrust
and remorseless hate.

(2)

Across the eons of our past,
we should ponder
the incalculable sum
of *potential life.*
What might have ever been,
but wasn't.
We are the tiny few of
the infinitesimal fraction
that ever came *to Be.*

Most who were born,
perished too early,
never experiencing
what we take to be
our natural right.

Condemned by
indifferent fate,
they could never touch
the gifts laid before us.
Unjustly cursed by
disease, violence,
poverty and disaster.

Few of us experience
long comfortable lives,
sheltered from ugliness.
Fewer still embrace
without hesitation,
the goodness and wonder
surrounding them.

Transfixed instead by what
is shallow and meaningless.
What is hard to recognize
until we see time is no longer
on our side.

(3)

Beyond all doubt and sorrow,
beyond the reach of our despair,
recognize devotion to goodness
is our weaker instinct.
Yet more profound than
our curse.

Beyond what is meaningless
and random.
The indifferent universe of irony
that blindly created us.
It is only through love and compassion.
Our desire to create beauty.
Our impulse for justice and betterment
that we find
the essence of righteousness.

We arose from the mystery of *Being.*
And somehow, through the flickering
of our weakest instinct, became
imbued with the eternal
that gave us birth.

We've slowly come to recognize
our mission is to rise above
the ugliness of existence.
To dismiss the moral vice
of eternal reward.

Instead, recognize even
in our despair,
what the ancient Hebrews
came to understand:
That we shall be as gods!

THE GOD GAME

I'm the vengeful instrument of God's darkness.
Praise and obedience are the parameters
in which I play.
Weakness is neither acknowledged
nor allowed.

The Kingdom of the One True God
is ruled Either/Or.
Life is nothing but reward
for those of faith,
and punishment
for those who dare stray.

Questions and doubts merely
the parlance of the weak.
Maybe and *perhaps* are
cancers weakening
our resolve.

Evil doers confuse us
with big words
and complex thoughts,
sowing doubt into our faith.
They want to bring us to our knees!
Secular humanism,
tolerance and diversity,
compassion and charity for all—
who are not like us.
Foreign ideas doom and
threaten the White God we serve.

I'm a bulwark against these nefarious hordes.
My AK-47 and hostile posturing,
symbols of Divine Retribution.
I am but one of the irrepressible
Christian soldiers,
who will destroy
all he's deemed Evil.

A codicil of our creed is
my surety.
Because God created me
in His Image,
my thoughts and actions
reflect his will.
How could it be otherwise?

So all my unspoken,
haunting fears
convey his distress,
calling me to action.
Violent thoughts and feelings
running electric through me,
resentment and disgust,
no doubt are decrees
of his displeasure.

And so,
all that differs from me,
all that opposes
and threatens me,
threatens my awesome God.

And yet beyond my surety
something gnaws away.
A fretting I can't escape.
Because there's a truth
I'll never confess:
I'm a covetous,
fearful creature
overwhelmed by desire
for power, righteousness,
licentious pleasures
that betray my faith.

I hate and fear all those
inferior to me.
Daring to challenge my beliefs,
expose my weaknesses.
For without my guns and brutality
I'd crumble beneath
this bewildering life.

And so I play the game of
God as Idol.
A desperate illusion I can
placate and flatter.
The temple where I hide
my impotence,
and build illusions of strength.

No matter what sins I commit
for the Glory of His Name,
the violence and cruelty
I'd gleefully inflict.
The forbidden indulgences
I might partake if
I should become so weak.

For in this game I cannot lose.
I need only lay prostrate
before Him.
Profess unwavering
love and devotion,
to be absolved
in *His Eyes.*
For in the scriptures
I was taught,
flattery and obedience
are surely what
He covets most.

YOM HA SHOA

I was born 10 years past the Holocaust.
In the decades that followed
shock and horror reverberated, from
what our evil does to one another.
Even antisemites for a while
vailed their animus towards us.

As a Jewish-Irish boy I was taught
to remember but hide my heritage.
Such ambivalence and confusion
living life with uncertain identity.
The quiet unease it brings.

The fatigue of constant vigilance,
for unguarded remarks
by friend or neighbor,
colleague or stranger.
Someday they may betray me
if there's a fickle change in
the Zeitgeist wind.

I worry such thoughts
might arise from the lips
of a lover.
That even they could
be *one of them.*

There's a chill living
in these nightmarish times,
when torch-lit fascists march
past synagogues chanting
Jews will not replace us!
Spewing lies of *globalist's*
conspiracies.
Jews, the masterminds of
Great White Replacement.

The slaughter of October 7th
became the tinnitus of dread.
The nightmares of youth
have returned.
Absurd rationalizations
we once told ourselves.
It won't happen here!
America is not Germany!
Rings more false than true.

Too-easily erased from
gentile minds,
pogrom horrors
only a few months old.
My Leftist allies betrayal
most loathsome of all.

So I the atheist
ambivalent Jew,
who lights his menorah
in a window,
no one else will see.

Who never forgets
the taunting skinheads
who once roamed the Haight.

Who's endures slights
with chiding humor.
Because *I want to belong
with everyone else!*

Today my somber mood beckons
to be among my people.
Reflecting the slaughter
of innocence.
Both Palestinian and Jew.

In the pall of sorrow and
hopelessness I carry.
With dread and futility I ask
the *Un-answering Absence:*
Why must our history
be so cyclical?

And I become the silence
that follows,
having known the answer
all too well.

So I the atheist Jew
with Irish eyes,
sits quietly in a temple.
In remembrance of
Yom Ha Shoa.

ELEGY FOR MARIA TRINIDAD

You were born a Summer's child
of the gods who made
the winds and golden hills.
Sister to the waving grasses,
and birds who sang as
you ran wild,
beneath billowed skies.

The only fear you'd ever known
was the dark clouds of angry gods
who'd roar and crack the skies
with bluish light.

But one day in the low of Autumn
a darker force arrives.
Strangers in shiny armor
surround your family.
A hooded man in black robes
steps towards you chanting
in a foreign tongue.
Above your head he holds
a cross on which a
tortured man is staked.

Driven into the valley
your spirit flees when
you see your neighbors
huddled in a beggarly stockade.
Behind them looms
a white building,
where soon you'll learn
lesser gods easily perish.

Winter comes cold with shame.
Your heart blackened by those
who teach you fear and self-loathing.
And for your soul's salvation
all memories of your gods and hills
are banished.
Making hopeless their return.

In Spring a fever comes for you.
Delirium and rigors rack
your soaking body.
Beckoned by your
moans and tears,
the grasses and birds of
the hills return unseen,
to sing inside your mind.

They guide you down
the darkened arbor
past Mission walls
of pallor-mortis.
Soft winds have come
to carry you back home,
So you may dwell once more
in endless Summer.
Lulled by the whispers
of your beloved hills.

Author's Note: The young native girl christened "*Maria Trinidad*" was the first of four thousand Mutsun natives to perish at the California Mission of San Juan Bautista. She died less than a year after she and her people were herded into its concentration camp. Most of the incarcerated inhabitants perished from diseases brought by the Spanish conquistadors. The small cemetery next to the mission has only 20 crosses; one rests atop the small grave of Maria Trinidad.

THE JOYS
OF RANTING

CURMUDGEON'S BATTLE CRY 2025!

It's the righteous curse of time you see,
to be old and dumped on
Life's day-old rack,
soon-to-expire,
use,
freeze
or discard by
such-and-such a date.

And I'm shocked!
SHOCKED!!
It's finally happening to me!
A fairytale Baby Boomer
never meant to age — at least
not in the sense of our heroes —
Janis, Jim and Jimmy —
may they rest in eternal
opiated peace.

And certainly not
in a crumbling way
that age has done
others dirty.

Youth seemed eternal
and hopeful
on the front end of things.
Before I was dragged
kicking and screaming,
dumped in the LaBrea
tar pit of responsibility.

And OMG!
Those tedious years
playing hide-and-seek
with my therapist
only to learn my childhood
WAS JUST A FRICKING NIGHTMARE!

Trapped in a world
surrounded by crazies,
pretending to be family.
And most of my teachers?
(Reader, what do you think?)
More than just maybe!!!!!
So at least my mishegoss
has a valid excuse.

"So back when I was young…"
(Reader: *Oh dear god!*
What's he now gonna say!)
I never could fathom
cranky old folk's kvetching away.
Bitter as quinine I seem to recall,
hunched-over crab people
criticizing everything,
by anyone younger
than the age of dirt.

How insufferable and tedious
their wretched minds and
mouths.
It was really too bad that
rigor mortis hit them last!

And how in my youth
I so earnestly vowed
my life would not
amble down that
miserable path
to Hell!
HA!!!!!!!!!!!!!!!!!!!!!!
But then YOU all came along
with the passing years.
Such temerity to come of age
only to see the fucked-up world
you've found.

But why on earth do you blame me?
You don't understand it was
the world I'd found?

So now, I'm gonna sally forth
at YOU
with my disdain!
(though you pray
a fatal embolism
soon comes my way).
Nevertheless, WTF!
is the negative anthem
I will brey!

Ya know, back in my day
our feminist's decried,
how we cast young women
as our sex toys.

Ah Ha!
But now their
nubile granddaughters
just love twerking.
Beckoning to be banged
like a screen door caught
in a nasty hurricane's fury.

Ya know, back in my day,
before cell phones
made us all slaves.
We'd go about our way,
with nary a schmuck who'd
text whist blocking
—the supermarket entry,
—the salad bar boxes,
—the sidewalks,
—the roadways
and least we forget
—the elevator doorways!

Maybe just maybe
they'll someday understand.
But think again Bub!
Who are we kidding?
These schmucks would text
while reading poetry!

And no rant should end
without a shout-out to those,
who compulsively post
every restaurant meal.
It's just food you F***'s!

But my better angels do
try to intercede:
Dude!
Chill!
Just be grateful they don't
post a pic when
it comes out
the other way!

So alas my sweet poem
must come to an end.
But my diatribe lives on
til I gasp that final breath
of my wrath.

So go ahead punks!
Carpe Diem! if you must
(have to go look it up).
Shake your heads
in gleeful disdain.
You're surely gonna have
deflating last words
that leave me
half-slain!
(READER: "OK BOOMER!!!")

VIEW FROM 30,000 FEET

If you're cursed to sit through
organizational meetings,
Your ears and mind
no doubt abused,
by grandiose aires of
the vaingloriously vacuous,
who trumpet their arrival at
the threshold of your mind.

They condescend to brush away
your considered thoughts.
Problems you see with
your un-lying eyes.

But in this inner sanctum of
a bubble-wrapped world,
C-Suite denizens bow
and scrape,
before the "North Star" of
organizational excellence
(or so they think).

They babble the lexicon
of pseudosensitive drivel,
that only an obtuse
HR department could
gleefully design.

These minion-minds of
immaculate misconceptions dismiss
your meticulous observations
in two snooty ways

First they try a genteel tact.
Rapt with fake concern with
a concealed fuck-off!
Thank-you for your thoughts.
Let's stick a pin in that!

Their more annoying approach
is their golden shower of contempt:
If you view the situation
(as we do)
from thirty thousand feet, you'll
clearly see that....
As if their panoramic view
holds the perfection of
knowledge and perception!

Deflated silence follows
your polite dismissal.
As the conference room
doors close behind you,
the un-trammeled half of
your prattle-wacked brain,
stops to ponder
their precarious wisdom.

You mutter to yourself
(and no-one else in particular):
But at thirty-thousand feet,
you can't see a fucking thing
happening on the ground!!!

THE IS OF WHAT IS:
AN ONTOLOGICAL INQUIRY

It is what it is
but what is It?
And what is the what
of what Is?
Stated differently,
Is what is It,
truly what Is?
So now we're dealing with
the ontology of IT and IS.

And let's set aside for a moment,
the WTF of whatever
the what of WHAT is?

It's all very confusing to me.
The WHAT,
The IS,
and the IT of WHAT is.

And Bill Clinton
certainly didn't help.
He fouled much more than
a sexy blue dress!
He totally screwed our minds
when he said:
*It depends upon what
the definition of Is, is!*

It all sounds very Eastern
and deeply hermetic to me.
So I turn to a mystic,
seeking enlightenment from
the Four Noble Truths, of
WHAT IS IT THAT IS?

With a smile of serenity
he softly replies:
Seek in the wisdom of
your lowest chakra.
There you may find
in deep contemplation,
where the Aum of IT
dances with the Om of IS.
WHAT IS, is no more than
what is revealed to you
as IT IS!

Getting nowhere swirling
like a Dervish, in this
silly circle of jerk.
I seek out a perspective
cross-culturally grounded,
hoping to find
another perspective.

It is what it is
Is no more than
It BE what IT BE.
But don't you
sorry-assed crackers
be expropriating culture
from me!
Now step-out of my face
before you become
the Wonder Bread of
IS of WHAT WAS!!

Perplexed and forlorn,
Adrift in this wretched
epistemological hell.
I turn to a philosopher
as my final desperate call.
It is what it is,
is that what
you're asking me?
The IS of what IT is?

Well! For you college kids
whom Latin wasn't
"really your thing",
It is simply:
HONOS and ESSE
HONOR WHAT IS!

REFLECTIONS, MOODS (PART 2)

Imagination, Magic
and Secondary Worlds

I've never asked about imagination's *what and why*. Long hours of my childhood were spent drawing and playing in the solitude of my bedroom. A world unto myself away from mundane motions and unsettling commotions of life outside. Among the gifts solitude bestows, the most important was creativity. A child's imagination permeates the world surrounding them. Children are by nature spiritually feral: instinctually governed by animism. They pour spirit into every object that speaks to them.

The *what and why* of our soul is an elusive archeology. Our early perceptions are inchoate interpretations of experience, because they've preceded language. For language gives form to thought. It guides our soul, fashions our memories and creates our narrative. And so, memory becomes inextricable from the story we're compelled to weave. The enigmas born in our pre-verbal world becomes part of the intangible we carry within us. This feral being conceals itself from us, but channels our perceptions and creativity in response to the world we both encounter.

I spent my Summers as a child on an isolated island in the Central Adirondack mountains, surrounded by other islands densely forested. The largest of these had an old fir tree that rose above the others. It stood out because its few remaining branches formed (in a young child's imagination) a tall, bearded creature. My eyes were always drawn to him. Without my understanding he became a beacon of familiarity; a sense of permanence a child's sense of security craves.

Anthropomorphism didn't stop with my tree-creature. The quiet mountains that loomed above the lake, and those far-off in lighter blues, exuded personality because of their distinctive shapes and rocky scars. And so did each boathouse and camp on the shores, when we ventured across the lake.

Like the tree-creature and the mountains, each of them exclaimed something ineffable. The part of me who uttered them never understood the why, because "he" withheld his secrets from me. And as my innocence waned, so did the magical world-within-the-world. Although the awe-struck child faded away, a residual of those magical experiences survived.

Magic is akin to the echo of our prenatal experience: being part of a greater presence whose warmth becomes the myth of Eternal Oneness. This primordial desire for union might also create our desire for secondary worlds. Yet, a darker side of the child's world exists: their lowly state of submission and pleasing those with power. Childhood is colored by the need to get away without leaving. To not disappear because of this abject state. Perhaps it's the echoing of these early experiences, that art becomes imbued with the magic of childhood.

Another truth is that we can apprehend the structures of color, form, sound and words. We can map-out neural pathways connecting our symbolic and cognitive centers; and these with the deeper structures of an ancient creature we inhabit. Just as the intricacies of art *might* explain what *likely* moves us, ultimately it can only brush against the formless and fleeting. The shadow that moves ghostly across a room. It cannot *ultimately* explain (in the first instance) *the why of needing to be moved*. In a poetic sense, our psychic essence becomes the *"first mover unmoved"*.

What eludes us as adults is the mystery of the paradoxical. We sense a presence that feels both far away, and yet within us: an orphaned part of our being. Perhaps, an echo of what we surrendered to become adults, and whose loss we bore in silence.

To possess *"the it"* of magic or art would seem, somehow, to defile it within our hearts. And to make it part of our base existence (our actuality), would be to lose forever the sanctuary of secondary worlds. Inevitably we must surrender to the harshness of reality. If we refuse, we will wither and perish into addiction or madness. But our secondary worlds must persist in some fashion, in some sanctuary; that as adults, we too *do not perish from the truth*.

THE EIDOLON OF NIGHT

Fairy tale stories are
told in whispers,
by mothers sending
their children off
to dream, under
the spell of
faraway worlds.

The words and stories
are long forgotten.
What endures are
mystical images of
exotic worlds, cast
from the imagination
of Edmund Dulac's eyes.

A bejeweled dark princess
from the Arabian nights,
lingers by a starry sea.
She holds a white bottle
with a magic potion,
waiting for someone
we cannot see.

The enchanted Snow Queen
with expectant eyes,
sits pale and lonely
upon her throne of ice,
below the swirling
Northern lights

And all his magic
shades of blue draw
down the children's eyes.

The Eidolon of Night
gazes at the dawn,
its lavender and
its fading stars.
Above the clouds she sits
on a mountain throne,
watching over all
the sleeping creatures,
who dwell in the
cypress forest below.

Dulac beguiles a child's dreams,
so they may wander into
a magical world.
One, they will never see.
But their enchantment
will live on, in
the deep springs
of early memory.

PRAIRE SKY

I belong to many Facebook
art sites.
Each day I pass through
so many images, that
catch my eye.
Unlike the hours I spend
in museum galleries,
I don't allow my eyes
to let the artist speak.

Instead I swipe through images,
detached in an aimless way.
Stopping only to place an emoji,
repost to my page, or
share with my artist friend.

I did this moments ago,
when *Prairie Sky* appeared
on my screen.
If I saw it in a gallery,
I would meditate for a spell.
Invite the image to linger.
Let the artist's interior world
share his secret.

A weathered farm house with
its dark-eyed window
staring back at me.
The narrow gray path bending
towards it lonelier,
than its shabby whiteness
hints of *vacancy*.

A billowing gray looms
above the ambivalence
of home —
an atmosphere of
changing moods.

Distant streaks of sorrowed orange.
The crest of clouds in fleeing
gray suggests the light
we cannot see.

All the poignant allegories,
the artist lets flow
through my mind,
if only I'd stop and gaze.

Nine hundred minutes fill
the monotony
of a common day.
My mind runs
through them all
with relentless speed.
The constant pace of
unconnected thoughts,
the flickered shadows of
feelings passing by.

Scrolling mirrors the habits
of a meandering day.
To see only what the eye
first catches,
and the mind is
too distracted
to see.

https://www.josephalleman.com/collections/164425

STOLEN PORTRAIT

What stirs inside comes to
the surface when the camera
focuses on us alone.
Who of our many dimensions
makes themselves known,
when we become the subject
of another's object.

Behind a camera
the artist sees falsity
and bides his time,
waiting for something true
to emerge.

Unnerved and defenseless,
the subject seeks a façade,
deflecting everyone from
seeing too clearly.

So many things pass-by the mind,
we never hold them back for long.
Momentary truth somehow
flashes across our face.
Thoughts, feelings and memories
converge in a stream.
What others only see
if they gaze at us sincerely.

But once the shutter clicks,
we become a perspective
in reverse.
No longer looking out, but
a spectator looking in,
discomposed,
by what our stolen soul
might say.

AWAKE AT 4 AM

I awake at 4 AM
in profound sadness.
Asking why my silent other
sent a dream,
of someone long gone,
who once meant
so much to me?
A dream to remind me
I am powerless to say
no more than goodbye!

Staring into the darkness
at 4AM is to find myself
between past and future.
But it feels like nowhere.
An unease that dreams
often bring.
A reimagined past told
in storied lies that hint
at a truth unseen.

Once my beloved
grandmother's ghost
visited me.
Her sad face framed in
evening light.
Her hazel eyes.
The softness of regret
in the words
she kept repeating:
I'm so sorry!
I'm so sorry!
And over the years,
I still can't fathom why.

I've been awakened from
the little deaths of
dreamless sleep.
Haunted and dazed
by emptiness.
The premonition of *Being*
without a soul.
A revving mind without thoughts.
A body unwilling to move.
A consciousness buried alive.
Brushing against Eternal quiet,
that patiently waits for me.

Yet I need the netherworlds
of sleep.
Its evocative dreams,
the enigmas it poses,
its sadness and passions,
and its hints of nagging regret.

In my morning ritual
I linger in the clarity
that comes with coffee,
when the haunting hour
has passed.
Trying to decipher meanings
that might not be there.
Grateful, to find myself
back in the realm
of common days.

BREAKING AND THE BROKEN

What breaks between us
is often healed, but vulnerable.
It's never quite the same.
What shatters is beyond repair.
Too many shards to make us
whole again —
as if that were possible.

In all relations rise inevitable
frictions between two selves,
who brush against occult
boundaries that lie within
each other.

Over time in those we love,
our differences rumble
in the night,
when all the elusive words
we've not yet spoken stay
silent.

And when our discontents
become no longer small,
and exasperation raves
inside us,
resentment swirls until,
the other becomes
an uninvited shadow
sleeping between us.

We are forlorn children vexed
by a fable told long ago.
Our elusive *other-half.*
The mystical *absent one*
to whom we *should* belong.
Instead we awake each day
and find ourselves bound to
a *changeling.*
Despite the doubts and
fissured affections,
the strong-in-love mend themselves,
resisting the fated small deaths
that come between them.

Faded love evades confrontation,
despite tormenting truth
that grows inside them.
Beneath their discontent is a subtext
the other never sees.
The secret weighing of joys and pain,
the cost of being tied to one another.
Until the day they've shattered,
and the unencumbered truth is
finally spoken.
Enough has become too much.

Brokenness is seeing no path forward,
and we become hollowed-out orphans
of our own deceptions.
Nothing remains except
the fatigue of empty habit.

In our sorrow we are forced
to confront a stark truth
of being human.
It's hard to find another
who can travel that
difficult path with us.

PALPABLE SORROWS

I carry the dullness of
disappointment.
An aura of bitterness
not my own.
But placed upon the boy,
once surrounded
by palpable sorrows.
Those of a woman's despair.
Lost in loneliness
and regret over her
empty marriage.

Too small to carry
her sadness.
Too naïve to understand
her misfortunes — One's
that were not his to heal.
Too innocent to carry her curse,
into the *cul de sac* of
his own pain.

I've moved through my years
seeking out the sadness
of other women's lives,
in which I could find a home.
Never understanding the knot
that no man could ever undo.

Living a lifetime,
with the maledictions
of a resentful ghost.
Mystified by my loyalty
to the omen, of
her disappointment.

THE POEM THAT AWAITS YOU

(for Martha Diaz)

There's only one response
the soul receives
when overrun by death.
It comes when tides of loss
retreat, and memory falls
gently upon
the one you loved.

Longing for those impoverished
moments when her attention
turned to you — alone.
Receiving what she could give.

And she, trying to overcome
her sorrows and burdens,
weighed down by failed hopes,
a young woman dreams,
for a life beyond
her reach.

In every mourning comes
a moment of entry.
When a poem that has waited
for this hour
finds you—
at the bottom of darkness.

I've also felt the pain
when time is stilled
in tedious grief.
Wandering through a world
suddenly strange to me.
And they in turn
pass by,
indifferent and unknowing.

Yet even these words may not
reach you,
and pass by grief
unnoticed.

But perhaps there are
others who will.
A remembrance by someone
known to her.
Their poignant turn-of-phrase
opens,
what is held too close,
and suddenly
her aliveness returns.

The one you loved a lifetime,
beyond the ambivalence—
that always followed.
For the deepest poems
that wash upon the soul,
are neither clean nor pure,
but real and honest.

And when love's irony
can be embraced, with
unencumbered truth,
a glimmer of joy will
meld with sorrow.
And healing rises up,
where she will build
a home
within you.

WANDERING ELSEWHERE

(1)

We can always flee to
another world.
Restless minds take us there.
A place far away
from where we are,
but still within ourselves.

Children flow so seamlessly
into the realm
of imagination.
Lost in the fantasies
their minds so easily weave.

Above our monotony's
whispering:
This really can't be so!
Float the legacies of
Once upon a time.

When the world's mysteries
enfolded us with stories,
that quietly made a home,
for enchantment to sleep
nestled by our side.

(2)

My restless mind awakes
each day, and finds the world
it wanders lacking.
And the voiceless within
moves in feelings...

There must be
an elsewhere,
somewhere
I can be more
than this!

I need to flee from
who I've become.
The endured life conceals
its cost,
until imagination grows
old and mad,
the soul quiets,
and suddenly — I'm lost.

Yet we're never far
from the portals of escape.
I've entered through
the swirling *"Starry Night."*
Fused with stoned memories.
Drifting away with
a phase-shifting guitar.
Calling me to float above
the mellotron's chorus,
and rise into the ethers
of elsewhere.

(3)

The *Paradox of Being* is
Existence
cannot be long endured,
without
a sanctuary for
imagined worlds.
And yet,
within us
is a boundary,
beyond which lies
a premonition
of terrors.
If we were to
let ourselves slip
away forever,
from the world
of familiarity.

SAMBA

Come back and feel
the fullness of life!
Let your heart return
to where it once lived.
Remember the music
that fueled passion, when
you were young, and
everything lay before you.
Leave what's died
within you
behind.

Remember the night
you saw *Black Orpheus,*
and a new world opened.
The unexpected gift of
nameless masses,
suffering beyond
what you could grasp.
The words that told
their plight.

There is no end to sadness.
Happiness never lasts.

Yet they rose above despair
in song and dance.

Samba's triumphal grace is
sadness and longing turning
to joyous beauty.
Touching the lightness
of renewal —
if only for a while.

Remember that night on
a beach in Bahia, as
your burdens vanished.
Laughing and splashing
in the shallows dancing,
Frevo you'd learned
that day.

Later wandering
the narrow streets
when you came upon
a pagôde party.
Their warmth and laughter.
The lilting music they sang.

And when they noticed you
outside their gate, with
a smile on your face.
How they welcomed you
like a neighbor,
to eat, sing and dance
into the dawn.

And how could you forget
the young morena dancing
care-free down
a cobblestone street.
Her swaying hips in a
tight white dress.
Arms raised to the sky.
Celebrating her youth and
the sensual night
to come.

And as she disappeared
in the dim light,
you imagined an
erotic liveliness
you'd never known.
If only you could've
been with her that night!

The joys of youth are
no longer yours.
But samba lives and never fades.
The adored music you
avoided for so long, and
still can't fathom why.

Samba reminds you
not to perish,
when your day-to-day
weighs you down.

Listen again!
Sing *A felicidade* in a place
your voice will echo.
Dance once again,
(in private if you like).
Be grateful for what
lifted you when
your best years
lay ahead.

Sway with all your sadness,
your joys and longings.
Let the music color
your colorless days.
It will always be
what you've loved most,
and yet forgotten.
Samba lives and never fades!

MAKANDURA

Living a tedious half-life of
dulled imagination.
Memories of unusual places I'd seen,
became no more than faded dreams.
Three pandemic years
surrounded by cancer, took me
from the beauty of other worlds.
And so, my desire for them
languished away.

I somehow made a journey
to Sri Lanka.
Hoping to find that sensation
of being fully alive.

An hour north of Colombo
sits a colonial mansion,
on the edge of a palm-treed lake.

Slanted light beamed
down through the trees,
waving shadows across
the white veranda.
Making the lawn more
vividly green,
and red blooms
more lucent
atop the spindly trees.

With warmth and grace,
I was guided down to
a gazebo near the shore,
Greeted with spiced food,
whose flavors
I'd never tasted.

Sated.
Reclined.
Surrounded by
flowering aromas and
lilting songs of exotic
birds rising above
the rustle of
swaying trees.

Lifted into the breeze
I drifted
away from those
shredded years.

And for a while,
I wandered in
the slowness of tranquility.
Cradled by the gentleness
of other worlds—
the ones that are real.